THE VICTORIAN HOUSE
Coloring Book

Illustrated by
Daniel Lewis

Written and Researched by
Kristin Helberg

Dover Publications, Inc.
New York

Published in Canada by General Publishing Company, Ltd., 30 Lesmill Road, Don Mills, Toronto, Ontario.
Published in the United Kingdom by Constable and Company, Ltd., 10 Orange Street, London WC2H 7EG.

The Victorian House Coloring Book is a new work, first published by Dover Publications, Inc., in 1980.

DOVER *Pictorial Archive* SERIES

The Victorian House Coloring Book belongs to the Dover Pictorial Archive Series. Up to four illustrations from it may be used in any one single publication without payment to or permission from the publisher. Wherever possible include a credit line, indicating title, authors and publisher. Please address the publisher for permission to make more extensive use of illustrations in this volume than that authorized above.
The reproduction of this book in whole is prohibited.

International Standard Book Number: 0-486-23908-X

Manufactured in the United States of America
Dover Publications, Inc.
180 Varick Street
New York, N.Y. 10014

INTRODUCTION

HAVE A FAVORITE PHOTOGRAPH. It is a picture of my father's room at college, around the beginning of this century. The photograph was professionally taken, and I have sometimes wondered why my father went to that trouble. I think I finally know. The room was not just any college room, it was a kind of miniature Victorian palace, containing a little of everything that the word "Victorian" suggests. And so you might say (considering it was not a particularly *large* room) that it was somewhat cluttered. "Overcrowded" would be more accurate.

It was a dark room with smallish windows, Gothic in style, and the furniture was heavy and elaborately carved. The walls and bed were almost buried beneath "hangings" of intricate and complicated patterns, each different from the others. There were brass tables from India, delicate vases from the Orient and knickknacks of every conceivable variety from every conceivable country. Pictures and portraits covered what was left of space on the walls. My father had presumably borrowed all of it from his father and mother to achieve the desired effect.

Which, I think, was to create the most romantic surroundings he could imagine. For that, to me at least, is what "Victorian" meant . . . an imaginary world reconstituted from some half-real, half-dreamed world or worlds of long ago and far away. Isn't it, after all, what all of us would like to do with our houses, to turn them into make-believe places where everything is strange and marvellous and beautiful and where we are always eternally happy? And so, whether we are in fact children or simply grownups who think like children (as I am), we decorate our rooms in fanciful ways so that we can at least *pretend* to live in a more wonderful world than perhaps we really do.

That's why I think the period of Victorian houses, and of the rooms within those houses, was surely one of the *most* fanciful in history. A Victorian house could transport you instantly and magically to just about any place you wanted to go.

So here we go on an adventure into the Victorian era! From the summertime land of the front porch, right up to the attic, chock full of wonderful rubbish.

What a trip you are about to take! I believe you are going to have a very good and interesting time. Bon Voyage!!

JOHN PHILIP SOUSA III
New York, December 3, 1979

THE
VICTORIAN HOUSE
Coloring Book

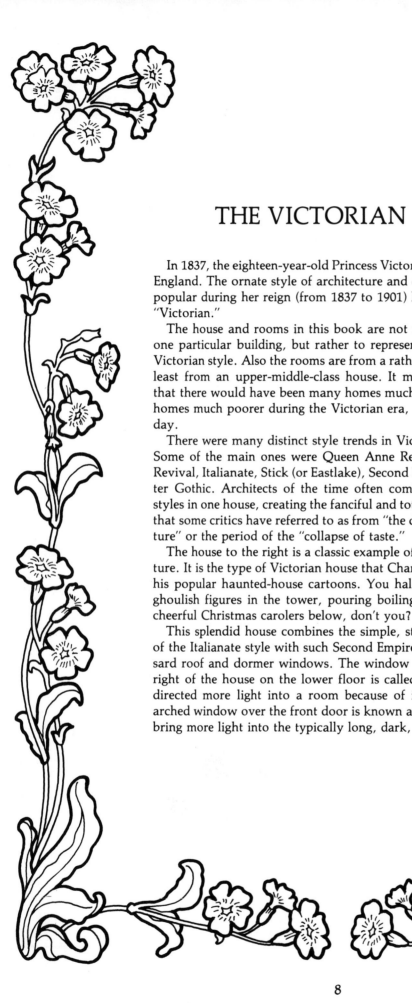

THE VICTORIAN ERA

In 1837, the eighteen-year-old Princess Victoria became Queen of England. The ornate style of architecture and decoration that was popular during her reign (from 1837 to 1901) has been designated "Victorian."

The house and rooms in this book are not meant to document one particular building, but rather to represent several phases of Victorian style. Also the rooms are from a rather grand lifestyle, at least from an upper-middle-class house. It must be remembered that there would have been many homes much grander and many homes much poorer during the Victorian era, just as there are today.

There were many distinct style trends in Victorian architecture. Some of the main ones were Queen Anne Revival, Romanesque Revival, Italianate, Stick (or Eastlake), Second Empire and Carpenter Gothic. Architects of the time often combined two or three styles in one house, creating the fanciful and totally original houses that some critics have referred to as from "the dark age of architecture" or the period of the "collapse of taste."

The house to the right is a classic example of Victorian architecture. It is the type of Victorian house that Charles Addams used in his popular haunted-house cartoons. You half expect to see two ghoulish figures in the tower, pouring boiling oil on a group of cheerful Christmas carolers below, don't you?

This splendid house combines the simple, straightforward lines of the Italianate style with such Second Empire features as a mansard roof and dormer windows. The window that projects to the right of the house on the lower floor is called a bay window. It directed more light into a room because of its three sides. The arched window over the front door is known as a fanlight. It helps bring more light into the typically long, dark, entrance hallway.

THE FRONT PORCH

The Victorians considered living outdoors to be very healthful. Most homes had front porches which became outdoor living rooms on warm spring and summer afternoons or evenings.

Wicker furniture and rocking chairs were popular. For large parties, they would even move out some of the parlor furniture and rugs!

House plants were placed outside on pedestal tables or on ornate plant stands similar to the one shown here.

Embellishment was so popular that delicately etched glass windows appeared in everyone's hallway doors.

The pace of life was much slower than it is now and Victorians would spend many summer evenings on their porches counting shooting stars and exchanging stories and gossip. The evening hours slipped away as the men puffed on cigars and the ladies and children sipped glasses of lemonade.

THE FRONT HALLWAY

For many years the hallway was considered a mere passageway or tunnel leading to more important rooms, but during the later years of the Victorian era, people started treating the hall as a room in itself.

The elaborate piece of furniture at the left is a settee combined with a hat rack and umbrella stand. It also has a mirror to help the ladies and gentlemen adjust their hats.

The walls are covered with family photographs and there is also a Currier and Ives lithograph displayed on the landing.

The runner carpet on the staircase is held in place by a series of metal rods.

The Victorians loved plants and vines and put them in every available corner, creating a mini-greenhouse in each room.

A typical craft for the lady of the house was the making of ruffled silk lampshades. Sometimes these shades were heavily decorated with beading or ribbons, making them look like fashionable ladies' hats.

THE PARLOR

The parlor or sitting room was the showplace of the Victorian house. There was usually a plush-covered round table in the center of the room similar to the one we see here. On the table is a display of tiny framed photos and a plate to hold calling cards. If visitors came to call and found no one at home, they would leave their calling cards with the maid to let the family know that they had been there.

Floral carpets were all the rage. It was the accepted style to combine many patterns together—even striped wallpaper with wild floral fabrics and carpets! The arms of the over-stuffed chair sport handmade lace doilies.

The Victorians covered their walls with paintings, prints and family portraits. Tiered whatnots like the one in the corner to the right of the window held additional souvenirs and mementos.

On the mantel of the elaborately carved Carrara marble fireplace you can see wax flowers under glass domes. A little seashell box sits on the piano. All were probably made by the lady of the house since dainty handicrafts were very popular with Victorian ladies.

The bay window has been turned into a small conservatory with ferns and trailing vines.

THE LIBRARY

The most serious room in a Victorian house was the library or study. It was here that the business of running the household was conducted. The large desk to the right holds books and ledgers for maintaining household records and accounts. Here the lady of the house would conduct her correspondence and enter additions to her diary, which was probably kept in one of the smaller drawers in the desk.

The elaborate bookcase to the left holds leather-bound editions of reference books, dictionaries and classics of literature. We see two books on the table, one of which is the family Bible in which it was the custom to enter family history on blank pages and flyleafs.

The photograph over the fireplace is undoubtedly of a relative, while the marble bust is of a classical scholar.

The fireplace is laid with wood, but coals were added later when the fire was hot enough for them to ignite. The coal was kept in the fanciful scuttle to the left of the fireplace. The comfortable armchairs were used for cozy reading in the afternoons and evenings.

The chandelier is lit by gas, whereas the lamps on the table and on the fireplace mantel are lit by kerosene. Gas was piped into homes for lighting, but it was commonly used in combination with kerosene lamps and candles. The crystal pendants on the kerosene lamps were functional as well as ornamental since they helped to intensify and reflect light.

THE DINING ROOM

The most outstanding feature of Victorian dining rooms was the sideboard. Although elaborately carved and heavily ornamented, the sideboard, seen to the left, served a practical purpose. The family silverware and table linens were stored in its drawers. The "Sunday best" china and crystal glasses were put on display on its shelves. Even the mirrors on the sideboard served the useful purpose of reflecting light from the candelabra.

During a large meal like Sunday dinner, the silver serving platters were arranged on the sideboard to keep the table uncluttered.

The window hangings in Victorian homes were often very complex arrangements of two and three layers of cloth, as shown here. The under-curtain of lightweight fabric like organdy allows light into the house. The outer-curtains, of a very heavy and dense velvet, were drawn shut at night to afford privacy and to help eliminate cold drafts. These drapes were so heavy that it often took two men to hang them up again after spring housecleaning.

Near the window is a Japanese scroll. During the latter part of the Victorian era, oriental objects were in great demand and screens, scrolls and wall-hangings as well as vases and jars began appearing in dining rooms and parlors.

THE KITCHEN

By the latter part of the Victorian era, the majority of kitchens had hot and cold running water, and sinks. Ice-boxes were just that —wooden cabinets with a shelf for blocks of ice to keep food cold.

Gas ovens were available but were not as popular as the old wood and coal stoves like the one pictured here which was hooked up to a hot water tank so there was no waiting for hot water.

The floor was wooden except for the tiled area around the stove to protect against fire. Kitchen floors were kept bare so that it was easy to clean them.

The wooden bucket on the floor near the sink was called the slop bucket and was the early version of the kitchen garbage can. Food scraps from the slop bucket would be worked into the garden soil.

To the right of the sink is a hand-roller towel, a continuous loop of linen that could be rolled as it became soiled. When it was completely soiled, the toweling was changed.

The big work table allowed the cook a place to prepare food comfortably and contained a drawer in which to store utensils and measuring cups.

THE GAZEBO AND FLOWER GARDEN

Fresh floral arrangements were considered a necessity in Victorian homes. The lady of the house raised a variety of flowers in her backyard. Here we see a large and rather grand garden. The gazebo provided a nice shaded area for admiring the garden on sunny days.

The Victorians' interest in flowers was not just restricted to love of their color and form. They also assigned various traits and meanings to each flower. When someone was presented with a special bouquet of flowers, all of the floral meanings fit together into a message. It was a rather formal era and people sometimes used flowers to express their feelings instead of verbalizing them.

Here is a list of the flowers and the meanings which Victorians assigned to them taken from *Flower Lore* by a Miss Carruthers of Inverness, published in 1879.

anemone: brevity
belladonna: fatal
camellia: excellence
carnation: admiration
cherry blossom: education
crocus: youthful gladness
daffodil: regard
daisy: innocence
edelweiss: daring, courage
fern: fascination
forget-me-not: forget me not
grass: usefulness
holly: good wishes
iris: hope
ivy: fidelity
lily of the valley: return of happiness

marigold: sorrow
mistletoe: surmounting difficulties
narcissus: egotism
olive: peace, security
pansy: thought
peach blossom: a bride
poppy: sleep, consolation
roses: passionate love
sunflower: pride, riches
sweet pea: departure
tulip: ardent love
violet: steadfastness
willow: forsaken love
zinnia: thoughts of absent friends

The illustration is on pages 24 and 25. Pages 23 and 26 have been left blank so that you can, if you wish, remove and display the large picture after coloring without damaging the rest of the book. Simply open up the two staples, remove the sheet and then reclose the staples.

THE MASTER BEDROOM

The massive Renaissance-style bedroom suite we see here is carved from walnut and walnut burl. Both the dresser and the night stand near the bed are topped with marble.

To the right of the bed is a photograph of a beloved uncle and above it hangs a reproduction of a painting by a popular nineteenth-century American artist.

In the foreground, near the armchair, is a fire screen that the lady of the household has been embroidering. The crocheted edges on the pillowcases are also her handiwork.

The richly embellished handwoven carpets are from Persia. The comforter on the bed is filled with goose down for warmth on cold, wintry nights.

THE DAUGHTER'S BEDROOM

Painted furniture was known as "cottage" furniture and was considered suitable only for informal use. The daughter's bedroom features a whole set of cottage furniture with each piece hand-painted and stenciled in a floral motif. The sleigh bed is set in a little alcove.

Victorian girls were encouraged to become versed in all the arts and handicrafts, not as part of some career, but to help make them cultured young ladies, hence the easel and watercolor set in this young lady's room.

Dollhouses were popular toys. Parents approved of dollhouse play because they felt it would help their daughters become organized and "house-proud" young women.

Popular, too, were dolls in all sizes made from all kinds of materials. The china or porcelain dolls were often "Sunday Dolls," kept in glass cases all week and only brought out on Sundays or holidays.

THE SON'S BEDROOM

Victorian parents were strict and demanding with their children. Rigid study and lessons were enforced each day except Sunday, when religious pursuits were encouraged. This little desk in this room is full of school books and papers.

Still, there was time to play. The rocking horse was a favorite toy in Victorian times, as it has been for centuries. Victorian boys, wearing paper hats and waving tiny swords, climbed on their horses and rocked off to imaginary battles. Tin soldiers were immensely popular, as were model train sets.

The bed, desk and chair show a strong Oriental influence in design. They are made of maple, carved and decorated to simulate bamboo.

THE BATHROOM

The first bathrooms were found only in upper-class homes because plumbing and fixtures were very expensive. Most Americans still used the old hip tub for their Sunday night baths, lugging buckets of hot and cold water to get the temperature just right. It's no wonder people took only one bath a week back then!

The bathtub pictured here is attached to an ornate gas water heater, thought by some to bring modern improvements to the bath. But these early gas contraptions had a nasty tendency to explode, causing prudent buyers to shy away from using them. Often, just cold water was piped into the bathroom and water was heated in the kitchen to be carried up for hot baths.

Victorian bathrooms were a joy to behold since they were often elaborately tiled like this one.

THE WATER CLOSET

The toilet or water closet (also called the "W.C.") was invented by an Englishman in 1596 but didn't really catch on in America until metal pipe became readily available in the 1860s.

The early toilets gave off an awful stench because the water trap had not been designed yet. The water trap is the ingenious turn in the toilet pipe which prevents the odoriferous sewer gas from working its way up into the house from below. Even with the water trap, many people thought it terribly unsanitary for the outhouse to be brought inside. They warned about the dangers of sewer gas, claiming that it caused untimely deaths! It was because of these fears that the toilet was separated from the bathroom in Victorian houses and placed in its own room: the water closet.

In keeping with fanciful Victorian design, the toilet was often decorated or sculptured, as this ornate model demonstrates.

J. BOLDING & SONS
PATENT SIPHON CISTERN

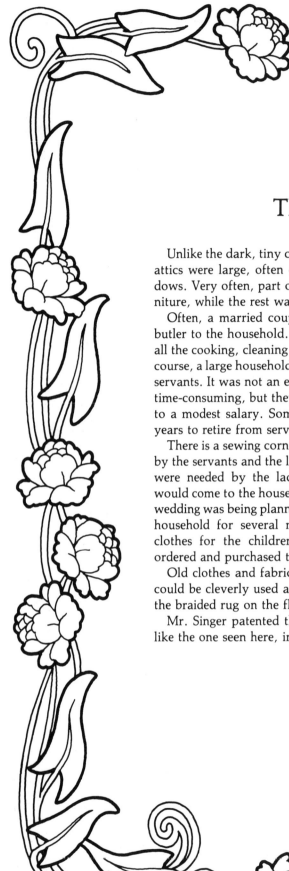

THE ATTIC

Unlike the dark, tiny crawl spaces we call attics today, Victorian attics were large, often comfortable areas, fairly well lit by windows. Very often, part of the attic was used to store rugs and furniture, while the rest was used as living quarters for the servants.

Often, a married couple would be hired to serve as cook and butler to the household. Between them, they were responsible for all the cooking, cleaning and general maintenance of the house. Of course, a large household would have employed more than just two servants. It was not an easy life, for their work was strenuous and time-consuming, but they were given room and board, in addition to a modest salary. Some couples saved enough money over the years to retire from service and start their own households.

There is a sewing corner in this attic. Routine mending was done by the servants and the ladies of the household. When new clothes were needed by the lady or her children, visiting seamstresses would come to the house to design and sew new apparel. If a grand wedding was being planned, seamstresses would often stay with the household for several months preparing the ladies' gowns and clothes for the children. Gentlemen and older boys generally ordered and purchased their clothes at a tailor's shop.

Old clothes and fabric scraps were never thrown away as they could be cleverly used again. Both the quilt on the brass bed and the braided rug on the floor are made from re-cycled fabrics.

Mr. Singer patented the foot-operated treadle sewing machine, like the one seen here, in 1851.

THE BASEMENT

Today we use our basements as catchalls to store all kinds of things that we are not currently using or that we intend to dispose of eventually. Sometimes part of the cellar is converted into a game room with a Ping-Pong table and dart boards.

The basement was a very practical area in the Victorian house. Very often a second wood and coal burning stove and a sink area were installed in the basement so the cook could preserve fruits and vegetables and bake during the summer without heating the rest of the house. You can see the neatly labeled jars of tomatoes, pickles, jellies and jams on the shelves.

This was also where all the clothes were washed and ironed. In 1858, Hamilton Smith patented the first mechanical washing machine. Until then, women had the back-breaking chore of scrubbing all clothes and linens by hand. Imagine trying to scrub out something as big as a bedsheet!

The funny-looking wooden tub with the iron wheel and handle on the top is an early type of washing machine. The top came off and soiled clothes, soap and hot water were put into the wooden tub. Then the top was lifted back on. The wheel was attached to revolving wooden paddles and when the handle was turned the paddles pushed the clothes through the water, forcing out the dirt. Next, the wet clothes were fed through the two rubber rolls of the bench-wringer you see here. As the handle was turned, the pressure would squeeze out the water, dropping the clean, damp clothes into the barrel on the other side. A strong arm was needed to turn the handles on both the washer and wringer. These machines were very hard on both the clothes and the washerwoman!

Ironing was also a chore. Though pretty much the same shape as today's irons, most old-fashioned irons were heated by being placed on a hot stovetop and a few by being filled with hot coals. It was hard to regulate the iron's heat. Women had to be very keen about continually testing the iron with a finger so it wouldn't scorch the fabric. Since the 'no-iron" miracle fabrics we have today didn't exist then, everything they washed had to be ironed!

THE CARRIAGE HOUSE

Just as we have garages today for our cars, the Victorians had carriage houses for their horses and buggies.

The carriage house was often a good-sized building and usually included a tiny apartment on the second floor to house the stable boy. It was the stable boy's job to feed and groom the horses, keep the buggy shiny and the horse stalls clean. Sometimes he also acted as the chauffeur.

There were automobiles in the late Victorian era but they were so rare that in the mid-1890s the Barnum & Bailey Circus displayed an auto as its main oddity. Even in 1900 there were only 8000 cars in use and roads were in such rough shape that it was a good many years until cars became practical.

In areas where there was often a lot of ice and snow, the family would own a sleigh to be used instead of a buggy during the winter months.

The cook's vegetable garden was located near the carriage house so the stable boy could work the hay and manure sweepings from the stables into the garden soil.

VICTORIAN RENOVATION

From about the 1920s up into the 1950s, most Americans didn't appreciate Victorian architecture. Many fine Victorian mansions and buildings were destroyed to be replaced by modern designs.

The year is 1935 and our once proud Victorian house stands deserted and in disrepair. The original owner has been dead for some time and the grandson who has inherited the house thinks of it as a "white elephant" and is only interested in the newer streamlined style known as Art Deco. He decides to put the house up for sale.

So, the lovely old building that has housed years of family reunions, births, weddings and holidays, stands silently in the moonlight for the next 15 years. The wind blows off some shutters, the roof begins to leak and local pranksters break some of the windows one Halloween night. The house is reputed to be haunted and the locals all avoid going near it at night and think the "For Sale" sign on the front lawn is a joke. "Who would be foolish enough to want that old hulk of a house," they say to each other. The grass grows taller and the stone fence tumbles down; it looks like our wonderful house is slated for demolition.

But, in the spring of 1950, a young architect is out on a country drive. He works in the big city and has been looking for a home in a small town nearby. Because no one wants a Victorian house, he is able to buy it for a very reasonable price and still have money left over to restore the house to its original splendor.

Although many homes were demolished, a new respect for Victorian architecture has grown in the past twenty years, and people have begun restoring them and cherishing them as the works of art they are.

BIBLIOGRAPHY

In order to produce this book, we did extensive research on Victorian architecture, interiors and times.

Some of the information we gleaned from books, while other facts were only discovered by visiting restored Victorian houses in the San Francisco Bay area.

Our book is a culmination of everything we saw and read, with a dash of imagination added. Here is a list of some of our favorite books uncovered in our search.

American Album, American Heritage Publishing Company, 1968.
Comstock, Helen. *American Furniture*, Viking Press, 1962.
Gabriel, Juri. *Victorian Furniture and Furnishings*, Grosset and Dunlap, 1971.
Gillon, Edmund V. *Victorian Houses*, Dover, 1973.
Hughes, George B. *Victorian Pottery and Porcelain*, Spring Books, 1967.
Maass, John. *The Gingerbread Age*, Rinehart, 1957.
Maass, John. *Victorian Home in America*, Hawthorn Books, 1972.
Peterson, Harold L. *Americans at Home*, Scribners, 1971.
Priestley, John B. *Victoria's Heyday*, Harper and Row, 1972.
Seale, William. *The Tasteful Interlude*, Praeger, 1975.
Waldhorn, Judith. *Victoria's Legacy*, 101 Productions, 1978.
Wood, Violet. *Victoriana, a Collector's Guide*, G. Bell, 1960.